The Little Book of BLEEPS

Excerpts from
The Award-Winning Motion Picture

What tHē βL∈∈P D̄θ wΣ (k)πow!?

In the Beginning was the VOID

Teeming with Infinite Possibilities

Of which You

Are One...

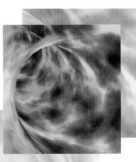

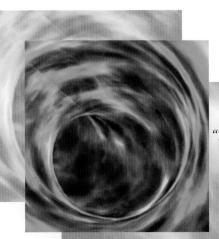

"The

    question is –

        how far

           down the

      rabbit hole of

   Mysteriousness

do you want

      to go?"

          –Reggie

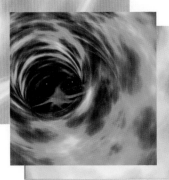

"Who are we?"

−Dr. Miceal Ledwith

"I am my atoms,

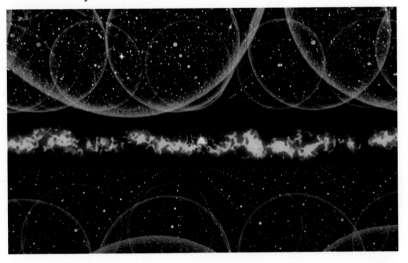

but I'm also my cells.

I'm also my macroscopic physiology. It's all true. They're just different levels of truth. The deepest level of truth uncovered by science and by philosophy is the fundamental truth of the unity. At that deepest subnuclear level of our reality, you and I are literally one."

–John Hagelin, Ph.D.

"What makes up things are not more things,
but what makes up things are ideas, concepts, information."
–Fred Alan Wolf, Ph.D.

"When we think of 'things,' then we make the Reality more concrete than it is. That's why we become stuck. We become stuck in the sameness of Reality, because if Reality is concrete, obviously I am insignificant. I can not really change it."

-Amit Goswami, Ph.D.

"If I change my mind, will I change my choices?
If I change my choices, will my life change?"
   -Dr. Joseph Dispenza

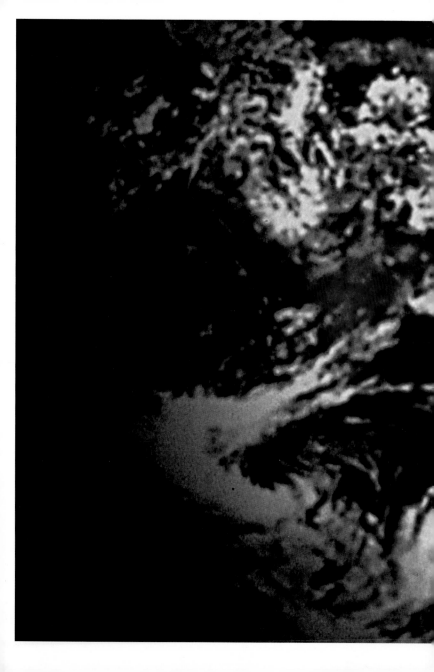

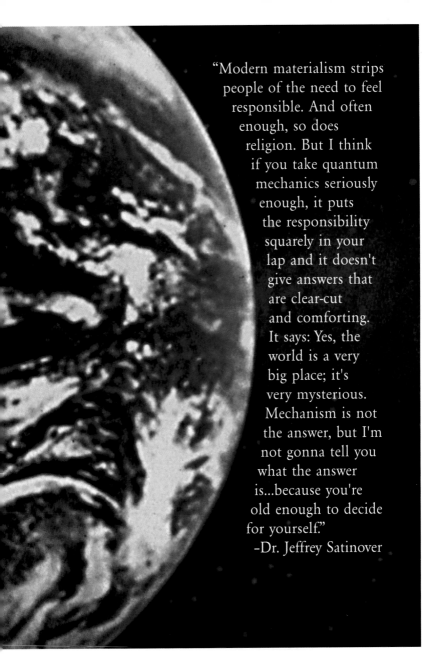

"Modern materialism strips people of the need to feel responsible. And often enough, so does religion. But I think if you take quantum mechanics seriously enough, it puts the responsibility squarely in your lap and it doesn't give answers that are clear-cut and comforting. It says: Yes, the world is a very big place; it's very mysterious. Mechanism is not the answer, but I'm not gonna tell you what the answer is...because you're old enough to decide for yourself."

-Dr. Jeffrey Satinover

"There is no God condemning people.
Everyone is God."
   –Ramtha

"When you ain't lookin', it's like a wave.

When you are lookin', it's like a particle."
-Fred Alan Wolf, Ph.D.

"How can you not friggin' SEE!?"
  –Amanda

"We're living in a world where all we see is the tip of the iceberg. The immense tip of a quantum mechanical iceberg."
     -John Hagelin, Ph.D.

"How can you continue to see the world as real if the self determining it to be real is intangible?"
     -Ramtha

"I think the more you look at quantum physics, the more mysterious and wondrous it becomes."
     -Dr. Stuart Hameroff

"There's this completely amazing magic
sitting right in front of your eyes."
-Dr. Jeffrey Satinover

"As far as whether we're just living in a big holodeck or not is a question that we don't necessarily have a good answer to. I think this is a big philosophical problem that we have to deal with, in terms of what science can say about our world, because we are always the observer in science."

    -Dr. Andrew Newberg

"In this infinite sea of potentials
that exist around us,
how come we keep recreating
the same realities?"
    –Dr. Joseph Dispenza

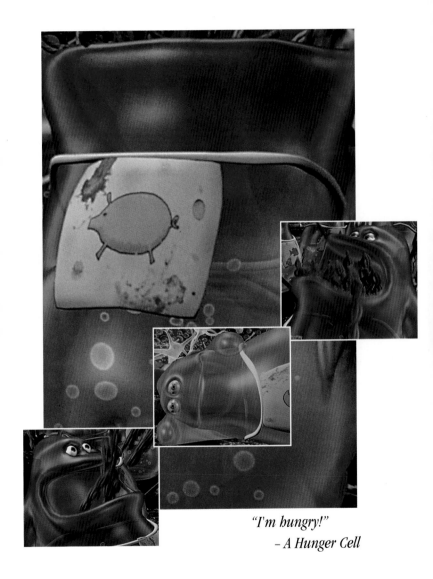

"I'm hungry!"
   – A Hunger Cell

"It's
very easy. Instead of thinking
of things as things, you have a habit. We
all have a habit of thinking that everything around
us is already a thing, existing without my input, without
my choice. You have to banish that kind of thinking...

Instead you really have to recognize that even the material world around us, the chairs, the tables, the room, the carpet, the camera included, all of these are nothing but possible movements of consciousness. And I'm choosing moment to moment out of those movements to bring my actual experience into manifestation. This is the only radical thinking that you need to do, but it is so radical. It's so difficult, because our tendency is that the world is already out there, independent of my experience.

It is not. Quantum Physics has been so clear about it. Heisenberg himself, codiscoverer of Quantum Physics, said atoms are not things. They're only tendencies. So, instead of thinking of things, you have to think of possibilities. There are possibilities of consciousness."

-Amit Goswami, Ph.D.

Yodo River, Osaka Prefecture
(water from Yodo River which pours into the Osaka Bay)
The Hidden Messages in Water, Dr. Masuro Emoto

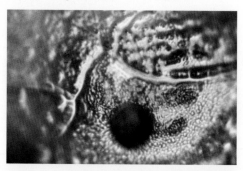

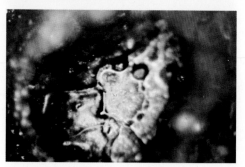

Water crystal from Fuiwara Dam before blessing
The Hidden Messages in Water, Dr. Masuro Emoto

"THANK YOU" The Hidden Messages in Water, Dr. Masuro Emoto

"Are people affecting the world of Reality that they see?
... You betcha, they are!"
    -Fred Alan Wolf, Ph.D.

Dr. Joseph Dispenza received his undergraduate training at Rutgers University where he majored in biochemistry. He received his Doctor of Chiropractic Degree at Life University. His continuing education has been in neurology, neurophysiology and brain function.

"Isn't it amazing that we have options and potentials that exist but we're unaware of them?"
– Dr. Joseph Dispenza

"I wake up in the morning, and I consciously create my day the way I want it to happen. Now, sometimes, because my mind is examining all the things that I need to get done it takes me a little bit to settle down and get to the point where I'm actually intentionally creating my day.

But here's the thing.

When I create my day, and out of nowhere, little things happen that are so unexplainable, I know that they are the process or the result of my creation. And the more I do that, the more I build a neural net in my brain and I accept that that's possible. It gives me the power and the incentive to do it the next day."

   –Dr. Joseph Dispenza

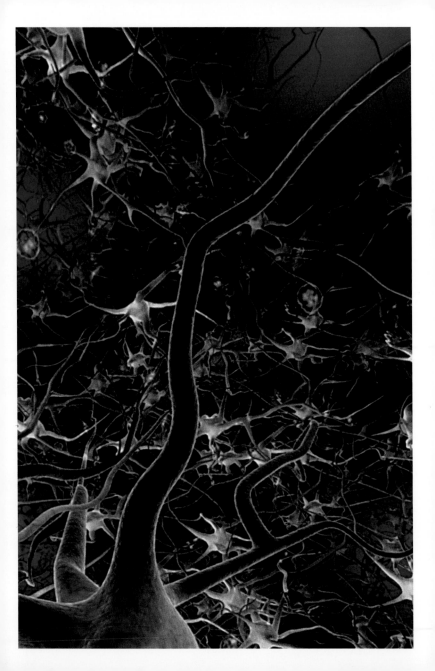

"The brain is capable of millions of different things. People should just learn how incredible we actually are, and how incredible our minds actually are. That not only do we have this unbelievable thing within our heads that can do so many things for us, and can help us learn, but it can also change and adapt, and it can make us better than what we actually are. It can actually help us to transcend ourselves."

–Andrew Newberg, Ph.D.

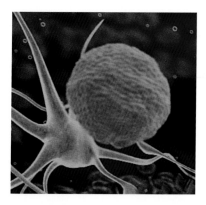

"Our mind literally
    creates our body."
    –Candace Pert, Ph.D.

"We build up models of how we see the world outside of us.

The more information we have, the more we refine our model one way or another.

What we ultimately do, is tell ourselves a story about what the outside world is."

–Daniel Monti, M.D.

Dr. Daniel Monti, M.D., received his Doctor of Medicine, summa cum laude, from The State University of New York at Buffalo School of Medicine in 1992. His Postdoctoral work was in the Research Scholars Program, Department of Psychiatry and Human Behavior, at Jefferson Medical College, Philadelphia, Pa. He is currently Chief of Complementary Medicine, Department of Psychiatry and Human Behavior, Jefferson Medical College, and Director of Mind-Body Medicine for the Myrna Brind Jefferson Center for Integrative Medicine, Thomas Jefferson University.

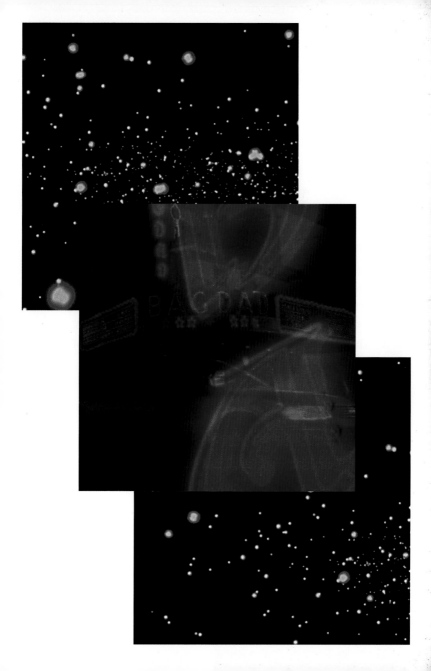

"If you accept with every rudiment of your being that you will walk on water, will it happen? Yes, it will! But you know it's like positive thinking. It's a wonderful idea, positive thinking, but what it usually means is that I have a little smear of positive thinking covering a whole mass of negative thinking, so thinking positive is not really thinking positive, it's just disguising the negative thinking that we have."

-Dr. Miceal Ledwith

"The science of how thoughts affect the molecules is unknown.

Water crystal from fountain in Lourdes, France. The Hidden Messages in Water, Dr. Masuro Emoto

Except to the water molecules, of course."
—Betsy the Tour Guide

"Your consciousness influences others around you.
   It influences material properties.
It influences your future.
   You are co-creating your future."
   –William Tiller, Ph.D.

"We like to think of
space as empty and
matter as solid.
But in fact, the truth
is almost exactly
the other way around."
-Dr. Jeffrey Satinover

Jeffrey Satinover, M.D. (psychiatry),
(www.satinover.com) M.S. (physics, doctoral
candidate in physics). Dr. Satinover is past
president of the C.G. Jung Foundation of
New York, a former Fellow in Psychiatry
and Child Psychiatry at Yale University and
William James Lecturer in Psychology and
Religion at Harvard University.

"Quantum mechanics allows
for the intangible phenomenon
of freedom to be woven into
human nature."

–Dr. Jeffrey Satinover

"But you've gotta really stop and think about what that means,

"The wacky, weird world
of quantum particles..."
–Ramtha

that's the same object and it's in two places at once."
-Dr. Jeffrey Satinover

"Superheroes use superposition…"
-Reggie

"We have to formulate what we want, be so concentrated on it, so focused on it, and so aware of it that we lose track of ourselves, we lose track of time, we lose track of our identity.

The moment we become so involved in the experience that we lose track of ourselves, we lose track of time, is the only picture that's real. Everybody's had the experience of making up their mind that they've wanted something.

That's Quantum Physics in action. That's manifesting reality"

-Dr. Joseph Dispenza

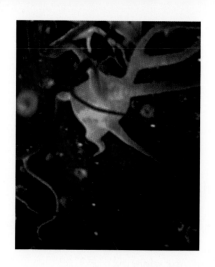

"The brain does not know the difference between what it sees and what it remembers."
    -Dr. Joseph Dispenza

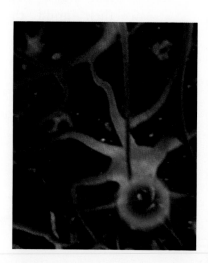

"She'll never fall for me…"
—Shy Cell

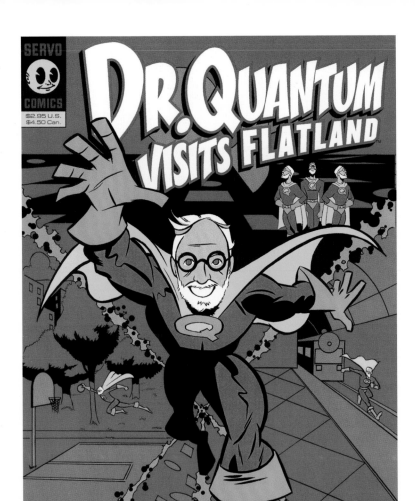

"Quantum Physics,
very succinctly speaking,
is the physics of possibilities."
        -Amit Goswami, Ph.D.

"We have the epitome of a great science. The closest science that has ever come to explaining Jesus' interpretation that the mustard seed was larger than the kingdom of heaven. The only science that can fit into that analogy is Quantum Physics.

Now we have great technology, from anti-gravity magnets to magnetic fields of zero point energy. We have all that, and we still have this ugly, superstitious, backwater concept of God."

   –Ramtha

Dr. Miceal Ledwith was Professor of Systematic Theology for sixteen years at Maynooth College in Ireland and subsequently served for ten years as President of the University.

"That I am at one with the great being that made me and brought me here and that formed the galaxies and the universes, etcetera, how did that get taken out of religion? It was not hard."

    –Dr. Miceal Ledwith

"I have no idea what God IS."
–Fred Alan Wolf, Ph.D.

"When I was younger, I had lots of ideas about what God was. And now I realize I'm not conscious enough to truly understand what that concept means."
–William Tiller, Ph.D.

"If I do this, I'm going to get punished by God. If I do the other thing, I'm going to get rewarded. This is a really poor description that tries to carve out a path in life for us to follow. But with deplorable results. Because there is really no such thing as good or bad. We're judging things far too superficially that way. Does that mean you're in favor of sin and licentiousness and depravity? No. It simply means that you need to improve your expression and understanding of what you're dealing with here.

There are things that I do, and I know they'll evolve me. There are other things that will not evolve me. But it's not good or bad. There's no God waiting to punish you because you did one or the other."
    -Dr. Miceal Ledwith

"Do I think you're bad?

I don't think you're bad.

Do I think you're good?

I don't think you're good either.

I think you're God."
-Ramtha

"Why can't I change?
What am I addicted to?

What will I lose that I'm chemically attached to? What person, place, thing, time or event, that I'm chemically attached to, do I not want to lose, because I may have to experience the chemical withdrawal from it?

Hence, the human drama."
  -Dr. Joseph Dispenza

"Does that mean emotions are good or emotions are bad? No. Emotions are designed so that they chemically reinforce something into long-term memory. That's why we have them."

  –Dr. Joseph Dispenza

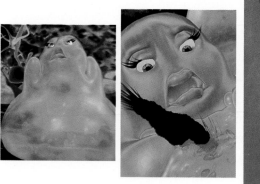

"Because all emotion is, is holographically imprinted chemicals."

  –Ramtha

Dr. Candace Pert, Ph.D., was awarded her Ph.D. in pharmacology, with distinction, in 1974 from the Johns Hopkins University School of Medicine. Dr. Pert conducted a National Institutes of Health (NIH) Postdoctoral Fellowship with the Department of Pharmacology at Johns Hopkins from 1974-1975. After 1975, she held a variety of research positions with the National Institutes of Health, and until 1987, served as Chief of the Section on Brain Biochemistry of the Clinical Neuroscience Branch of the National Institute of Mental Health (NIMH).

"The relevant search command that's going on is related to finding a certain emotional state. I mean, we can't even direct our eyes without an emotional aspect to it."

    –Candace Pert, Ph.D.

"Have you ever seen yourself through the eyes of someone else that you have become?

What an initiation.

Have you ever stopped for a moment and looked at yourself through the eyes of the ultimate Observer?"

  -Ramtha

"The average person considers their life boring or uninspiring because they've made little or no attempt to gain knowledge and information that will inspire them. They're so hypnotized by their environment — through the media, through television, through unattainable ideals of physical appearance, beauty and valor that everybody struggles to become but cannot — that most people surrender and live their lives in mediocrity. And they may live those lives, and their souls, their desires, may never really rise to the surface. So, they may want to be something else.

But if they do rise to the surface, and people ask themselves, Is there something more, or Why am I here? What is the purpose of life? Where am I going? What happens when I die? When they start to ask those questions, they start to flirt and interact with the perception that they may be having a nervous breakdown, and in Reality, their old concept of how they viewed their life and the world starts to fall apart."

    -Dr. Joseph Dispenza

"What I thought was unreal now, for me,

seems in some ways

to be more real

than what I think to be real,

which seems now more to be unreal."
 -Fred Alan Wolf, Ph.D.

"There were philosophers in the past who have said, Look, if I kick a rock and I hurt my toe, that's real. I felt that, it feels real, it's vivid, that means that it's Reality. But it's still an experience and it's still this person's perception of it being real."
   –Dr. Andrew Newberg

"Are all realities existing simultaneously?"
- Ramtha

"Most people don't affect Reality in a consistent substantial way, because they don't believe they can. They write an intention and then they erase it because they think that's silly. I mean, I can't do that. And then they write it again, and then they erase it. So, time average, it's a very small effect. And it really comes down to the fact that they believe they can't do it."
   –William Tiller, Ph.D.

"Makes you wonder, doesn't it...
If thoughts can do that to water...

"YOU MAKE ME SICK. I WILL KILL YOU"
The Hidden Messages in Water Dr. Masuro Emoto

Imagine what our thoughts do to us."
—Man in subway

"Everything around us is already a thing, existing without my input, without my choice. You have to banish that kind of thinking."

-Amit Goswami, Ph.D.

"Our bodies are 90% water."
—Betsy, Tour Guide

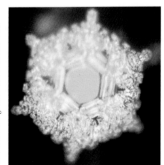

"Absolutely. Thought alone can completely change the body."

-Candace Pert, Ph.D.

"A receptor that has a peptide sitting in it changes the cell in many ways. It sets off a whole cascade of biochemical events, some of which wind up with changes in the actual nucleus of the cell.

Each cell is definitely alive and each cell has a consciousness, particularly if we define consciousness as the point of view of an observer."

    –Candace Pert, Ph.D.

"I am my cells."
    –John Hagelin, Ph.D.

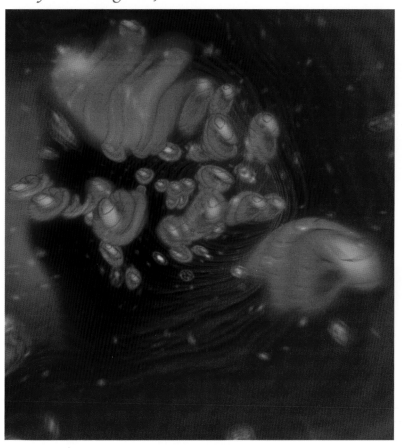

"We're reality-producing machines."
    –Dr. Joseph Dispenza

"I'll stick my ass in the cocktail sauce if I damn well please."
    —Sister of the Bride

"We bring to ourselves situations that will fulfill the biochemical cravings of the cells of our body."

    -Dr. Joseph Dispenza

"We are emotions and emotions are us. Again, I can't separate emotions. When you consider that every aspect of your digestion, every sphincter that opens and closes, every group of cells that come in for nourishment and then move out to heal something or repair something, are all under the influence of the molecules of emotion, I mean, it's this total buzz."

- Candace Pert, Ph.D.

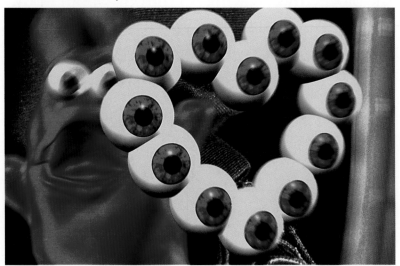

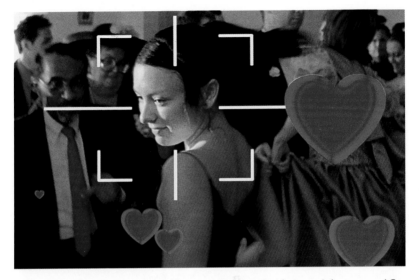

"So how can anyone really say they're in love with a specific person? They're only in love with the anticipation of the emotions they are addicted to. The same person could fall out of favor the next week by not complying.

My goodness, doesn't that change the landscape of our emotional outlook on personal needs and identities?"

        –Ramtha

"I am much more than I think I am.
I can be much more even than that.
I can influence my environment.
The people.
I can influence space itself.
I can influence the future.
I am responsible for all those things.
I and the surround are not separate.
They're part of one.
I'm connected to it all.
I'm not alone."

-William Tiller, Ph.D.

"We're consciously designing our destiny. We're consciously, from a spiritual standpoint, throwing in the idea that our thoughts can affect our Reality or affect our life, because Reality equals life. I have this little pact when I create my day. I say, I'm taking this time to create my day, and I'm infecting

the Quantum Field. Now, if it is in fact, the Observer watching me the whole time I'm doing this, and there is a spiritual aspect to myself, then show me a sign today, that you paid attention to any one of these things I created. Bring them in a way I won't expect, so that I'm surprised at my ability to experience these things, and make it apparent that it has come from you."

-Dr. Joseph Dispenza

"You are a God in the making, and you must walk this path. But some day you must love the abstract more than you love the condition of addiction."

-Ramtha

"How can we measure the effects? We get to live our lives, and see then, if somewhere in our lives, something's changed. Then, if it has changed, we become the scientists through our lives, which is the whole reason we're here."

   -Dr. Joseph Dispenza

Stuart Hameroff, M.D.,
(www.quantumconsciousness.org) is a Professor
in the Departments of Anesthesiology and
Psychology, and Director of the Center for
Consciousness Studies at the University of
Arizona in Tucson.

"I think the more you
look at quantum physics,
the more mysterious and
wondrous it becomes."
    -Dr. Stuart Hameroff

"Why are we here?"
    –Dr. Stuart Hameroff

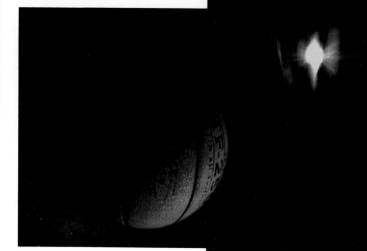

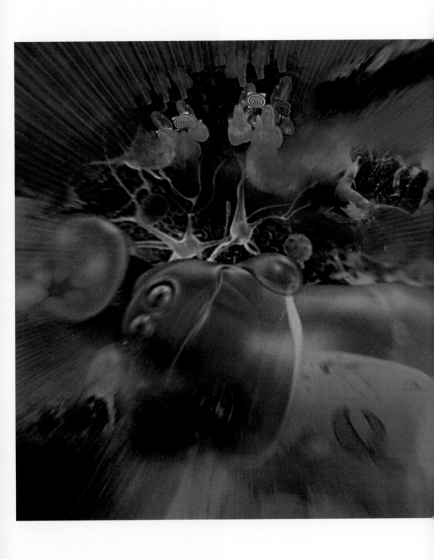

"We must pursue knowledge without any interference of our addictions.

And if we can do that, we will manifest knowledge in Reality and our bodies will experience it in new ways, in new chemistry, in new holograms.

New elsewheres of thought, beyond our wildest dreams."
        –Ramtha

"Have you ever thought about what thoughts are made of?"
   –John Hagelin, Ph.D.

"Oh, make me suffer.
I wanna hurt."
                    —Victim Cell

"God is a super position of all the spirit from all things."
                                        –William Tiller, Ph.D.

"Is there a possibility that all potentials exist side by side?"
   -Ramtha

"How can any man or woman sin against such a greatness of mind? How can any one little carbon unit on Earth, in the backwaters of the Milky Way, indeed, the boondocks, betray God Almighty?

That is impossible."
   -Ramtha

"Okay, guys. It's time for a course correction on our trajectory along the path of our adventure, and that course correction is the movement to a new paradigm. It's just an expansion of the old. It just says the universe is larger than we thought it was in our modeling and it's always larger than we think it is."
    –William Tiller, Ph.D.

Amit Goswami earned his Ph.D. from Calcutta University in theoretical nuclear physics in 1964 and has been a professor of physics at the University of Oregon since 1968. He taught physics for 32 years in this country, mostly at Oregon. Goswami is a senior scholar in residence at the Institute of Noetic Sciences and teaches regularly at the Holmes Institute in Los Angeles; UNIPAZ in Brazil; and The Theosophical Society in Wheaton, Illinois.

"But if Reality is my possibility, possibility of consciousness itself, then immediately comes the question of how can I change it? How can I make it better? How can I make it happier?"

- Amit Goswami, PhD.

"No one has ever come along and ever given you sufficient, intelligent knowledge about your beautiful self. How you work from the inside out.

Why you have addictions. Because you have nothing better. You have dreamt nothing better."

　　　　　–Ramtha

"Every age, every generation has its built-in assumptions, that the world is flat, that the world is round."

-John Hagelin, Ph.D.

John Hagelin, Ph.D., (www.hagelin.org) Dr. Hagelin holds an A.B. summa cum laude from Dartmouth College and an M.A. and Ph.D. from Harvard University. He is currently Professor of Physics and Director of the Institute of Science, Technology and Public Policy at Maharishi University of Management. Dr. Hagelin has conducted pioneering research at CERN (the European Center for Particle Physics) and SLAC (the Stanford Linear Accelerator Center) and is responsible for the development of a highly successful grand unified field theory based on the Superstring. In recognition of his outstanding achievements, Dr. Hagelin was named winner of the prestigious Kilby Award, which recognizes scientists who have made "major contributions to society through their applied research in the fields of science and technology." The award recognized Dr. Hagelin as "a scientist in the tradition of Einstein, Jeans, Bohr and Eddington."

"We're living in a world where all we see is the tip of the iceberg. The immense tip of a quantum mechanical iceberg."

-John Hagelin, Ph.D

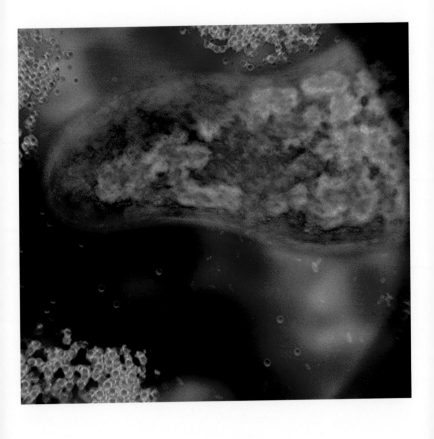

"Is it possible that we're so conditioned to our daily lives, so conditioned to the way we create our lives, that we buy the idea that we have no control at all?

We've been conditioned to believe that the external world is more real than the internal world. This new model of science says just the opposite.

It says what's happening within us will create what's happening outside of us."
    –Dr. Joseph Dispenza

"I guess it all depends on what you think is real."

—Jennifer

"Well, the way our brain is wired, we only see what we believe is possible. We match patterns that already exist within ourselves through conditioning."

– Candace Pert, Ph.D.

"When I talk about, we disappearing, I don't mean that we physically disappear. What I mean is that we move out of the area of the brain that has to do with our association to people...that has to do with our association to places, our association to things and times and events. We don't exist in the associative centers in our brain that reaffirm our identity, reaffirm our personality."

   -Dr. Joseph Dispenza

"Why do we keep having the same relationships?

Why do we keep getting the same jobs over and over again?"

-Dr. Joseph Dispenza

"Is everyone a mystery?
Is everyone an enigma?
They most certainly are."
    -Ramtha

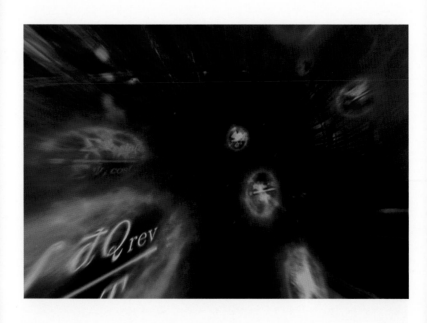

"Quantum mechanics allows for the intangible phenomenon of freedom to be woven into human nature."

-Dr. Jeffrey Satinover

"But if Reality is my possibility, possibility of consciousness itself, then immediately comes the question of how can I change it? How can I make it better? How can I make it happier? You see how we are extending the images of ourselves. In the old thinking, I cannot change anything, because I don't have any role at all, in Reality. Reality is already there. It's material objects moving in their own way, from deterministic laws, and mathematics determining what they will do in a given situation. In the experience, I have no role at all.

In the new view, yes, mathematics can give us something. It gives us the possibilities that all this movement can assume. But it cannot give us the actual experience that I'll be having in my consciousness. I choose that experience, and therefore, literally, I create my own Reality.

It may sound like a tremendous bombastic claim by some New Ager, without any understanding of physics whatsoever, but really, Quantum Physics is telling us that."
    -Amit Goswami, Ph.D.

"It's only in conscious
Experience that it seems that
We move forward in time.
In quantum theory,
You can also
Go backwards in time."
-Dr. Stuart Hameroff

"Don't just take it at face value,
test it out and see whether it's true."
      -Dr. Jeffrey Satinover

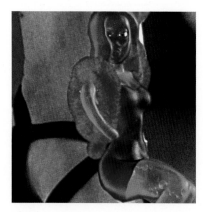

"Hi there, honey!"
—Lust Cell

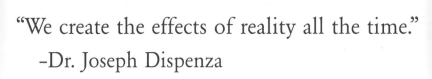

"We create the effects of reality all the time."
   -Dr. Joseph Dispenza

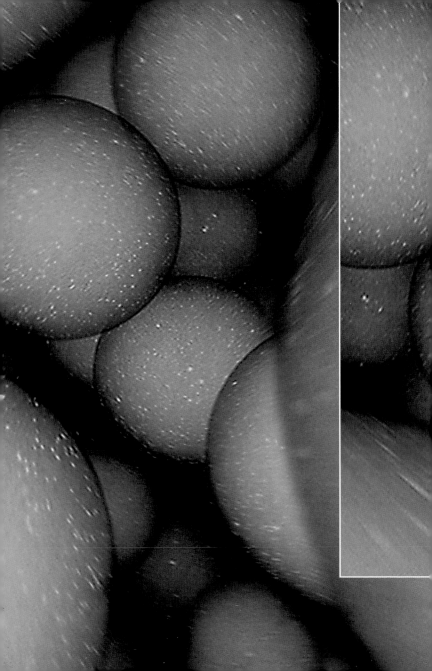

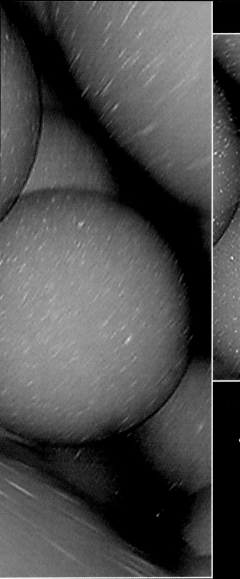
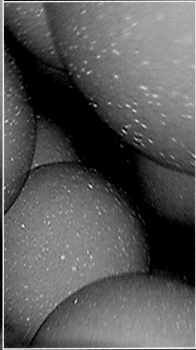

"Where do we come from?"
–Dr. Miceal Ledwith

"So you ask if emotions are bad. Emotions are not bad. They're life. They color the richness of our lives. It's our addiction that's the problem.

The thing that most people don't realize is that when they understand that they are addicted to emotions, it's not just psychological, it's biochemical.

Think about this.

Heroin uses the same receptor mechanisms on the cells that our emotional chemicals use.

It's easy to see, then, that if we can be addicted to heroin, then we can be addicted to any neuropeptide, any emotion."
    -Dr. Joseph Dispenza

Ramtha (www.ramtha.com). Ramtha is an entity channeled by JZ Knight. Master teacher at The Ramtha School of Enlightenment.

"The only way I will ever be great to myself is not what I do to my body, but what I do to my mind."

    –Ramtha

"Knowing that there's this interconnectedness of the universe, that we are all interconnected and that we are connected to the universe at its fundamental level, I think is as good an explanation for spirituality as there is."

-Dr. Stuart Hameroff

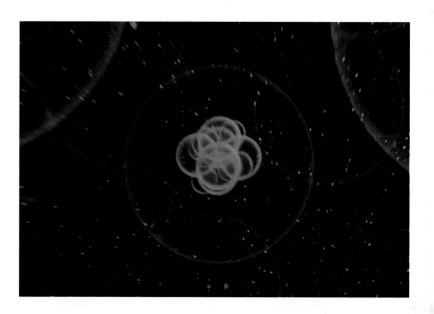

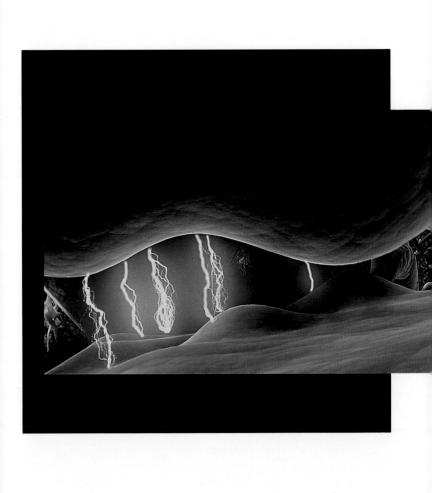

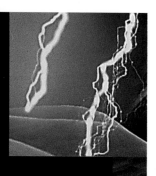

"We're in completely new territory, in our brain, and because we're in completely new territory, we're rewiring the brain, literally, reconnecting to a new concept, and ultimately, it changes us from the inside out."

-Dr. Joseph Dispenza

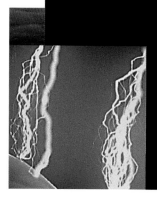

"Here we are actually filming great thinkers. Everyone in this room is a great thinker, now that we've got 'em thinking. That's always a trick, isn't it?"

–Ramtha

"Where are we going?"
–Dr. Miceal Ledwith

"To acknowledge the quantum self,
   to acknowledge the place where you rarely have choice,
   to acknowledge mind...
   when that shift of perspective takes place,
   we say that somebody has been enlightened."
   –Amit Goswami, Ph.D.

Fred Alan Wolf, Ph.D., (www.fredalanwolf.com) is a physicist, writer, and lecturer who earned his Ph.D. in theoretical physics at UCLA in 1963. His work in quantum physics and consciousness is well known through his popular and scientific writing. He is the author of ten books.

"There is no 'out there' out there, independent of what's going on 'in here' in here."

-Fred Alan Wolf, Ph.D.

"I have no idea what God is. Yet, I have an experience that God is. There is something very real about this presence called God, although I have no idea how to define God, to see God as a person or a thing. I can't seem to do it.

It's kind of like asking a human being to explain what God is. It's similar to asking a fish to explain the water in which the fish swims."

-Fred Alan Wolf, Ph.D.

"Asking yourself these deeper questions opens up new ways of being in the world. It brings in a breath of fresh air. It makes life more joyful. The real trick to life is not to be in the know, but be in the mystery."

- Fred Alan Wolf, Ph.D.

Andrew B. Newberg, M.D., is currently an Assistant Professor in the Department of Radiology at the Hospital of the University of Pennsylvania and is a staff physician in Nuclear Medicine. Dr. Newberg has been particularly involved in the study of mystical and religious experiences as well as the more general mind/body relationship in both the clinical and research aspects of his career. He has presented his work at scientific and religious meetings throughout the world and has appeared on Good Morning America, ABC World News Tonight, as well as periodicals including Newsweek, The New Scientist and the National Catholic Reporter.

"The brain is capable of millions of different things. It can take us to a higher level of our existence, where we can actually understand the world in a deeper way, where we can understand our relationship to things and people in a deeper way, and we can ultimately make more meaning for ourselves and our world.

We can show that there's a spiritual part of our brain, it's a part that we all can have access to, and it's something that we can all do."

    -Dr. Andrew Newberg

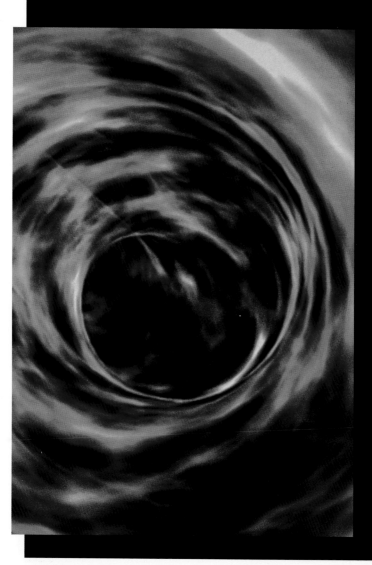

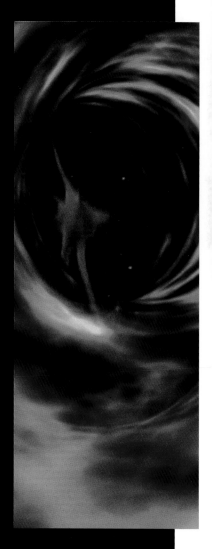

"You can't explain it, and anybody who spends too much time trying to explain it is likely to get lost forever down the rabbit hole of mysteriousness."

-Dr. Jeffrey Satinover

"My definition of an addiction is quite simple.
It's something you can't stop."
    –Dr. Joseph Dispenza

William Tiller, Ph.D., (www.tiller.org) graduated with a B.A.Sc. in 1952 with a degree in Engineering Physics from the University of Toronto. He also has an M.A.Sc. and a Ph.D. from the University of Toronto. Dr. Tiller has been a professor at Stanford University in the Department of materials science and Engineering. He has been a consultant to government and industry in the fields of metallurgy and solid-state physics and formerly Associate Editor of 2 scientific journals. He has published more than 250 scientific papers, three technical books and has five patents issued.

"All of us one day will reach the level of the avatars that we have read about in history, the Buddhas, and the Jesuses."
   -William Tiller, Ph.D.

"We always perceive something after reflection in the mirror of memory."
    -Amit Goswami, Ph.D.

"We know what an Observer does, from a point of view of Quantum Physics. But we don't know who or what the Observer actually is.

It doesn't mean we haven't tried to find an answer. We've looked. We've gone inside of your head.

We've gone into every orifice you have, to find something called an Observer, and there's nobody home. There's nobody in the brain. There's nobody in the cortical regions of the brain. There's nobody in the sub-cortical regions, or the limbic regions of the brain. There's nobody there called an Observer. And yet, we all have this experience of being something called an Observer, observing the world out there."

-Fred Alan Wolf, Ph.D.

"...and out of nowhere, little things happen."
-Dr. Joseph Dispenza

"Ponder that for a while."
–Fred Alan Wolf, Ph.D.

The Little Book of BLEEPS.